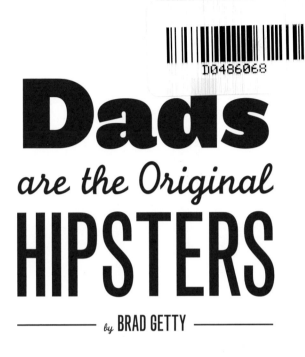

Dads

are the Original

HIPSTERS

— *by* BRAD GETTY —

CHRONICLE BOOKS

SAN FRANCISCO

Introduction

I have worse news than a PBR and skinny jean shortage for all the hipsters of the world. You are not original.

I know you'd like to believe that you were the first person to ever ironically wear a T, slip into skinny jeans, ride a bike, shoot film, go to art school, live apathetically, or drink cheap beer.

But you're not.

You've been subconsciously copying a legend with everything that you do and it's time he got the credit he deserved.

Your dad was the original hipster.

He made cheap beer cool, he rode a fixie, his jeans were tight, his T-shirts were deep Vs, and he partied harder than you can ever imagine. He was a hipster before being a hipster was a thing and he's been killing it since back in the day.

Your dad had style before you did . . .

Your dad had style before you did, seriously. Your brain's underdeveloped fashion cortex couldn't process his polish when you were a kid, so you ignorantly made fun of his clothes. But he knew how to put it on back then. He was walking sex appeal in a careful combination of threads. While you were parachuting your pants or wearing everything backward, he was suited up, skinnied down, and buttoned into the freshest wears on the streets. He had street style before it was a thing and he will always be the king shit of getting dapper.

Chukka Boots

Your dad wore desert chukka boots before you did and he has the distressed leather to prove it. As a world traveler, he bartered in Kolkata's outdoor flea markets, went on safari in Africa, and hiked mountains in the Swiss Alps. Most shoes couldn't withstand the wanderlust that your father's feet had, which is why he needed a boot that was comfortable, durable, and suave enough to help him charm a new mistress in every foreign land his feet touched.

SO HIPSTERS, next time you're lacing up your boots to go with your unwashed, ripped Levi's and a vintage Salvation Army shirt, remember this . . .

You couldn't walk a mile in your dad's chukkas.

Knit Hat

Your dad rocked knit caps before you did and he's got the matted-down man-fro to prove it. His weather-appropriate dome-piece changed the course of frigid fashion and turned a head sock into a runway must-have.

SO HIPSTERS, next time you're pulling a knit cap on in the middle of summer and letting the front bit of your unwashed hair peek out, remember this . . .

Your dad knew the seasons of style and he would slap the winter off your July head for disrespecting the laws of looking weather-appropriately good.

P.S. Your contribution to cold weather style was the headband and how many of those do you still see around?

Boat Shoes

Your dad wore Top-Siders before you did and he's got the white non-marking soles to prove it. He was a land sailor of the blacktop sea whose fresh footwear was Poseidon-inspired. They gave him sure feet in slippery conditions and man-anchored him to the ground so he could help your mom traverse treacherously slick surfaces.

SO HIPSTERS, next time you're toe-deep in boat shoes and not sliding across the beer-soaked dive bar floor, remember this . . .

Your dad wore socks with his Sperrys, unlike you, because women don't like men whose feet smell like they're homeless.

Cycling Caps

Your dad donned cycling caps before you did and he has the sweat-filled brim to prove it. Back when Lance Armstrong was swinging two-deep and Velocity was only a term used to reference speed, your dad was hyping bike brands on his head. He would flip the shit out of that brim so all the pedal honeys could see his laser gaze. He was raw, unbridled, rolling seduction that left a contrail of masculinity with every pedal push.

SO HIPSTERS, next time you're crotch up to a bike seat, flashing velo gang colors on the brim of your "trying too hard to be original" hat, remember this . . .

Your dad was the king of cycling and that cap was his crown.

Big Sunglasses

Your dad kept out hater rays with big shades before you did and he's got the oversized eye socket tan lines to prove it. His beta-blockers let his wandering eyes cruise the beach undetected. Like the dirty prince of summer, he stealthily grabbed eyefuls of apple bottoms.

SO HIPSTERS, when you're putting on your plastic-framed glasses to protect your bloodshot hungover eyes from the bright evil rays of the sun, remember this . . .

Your dad knew that the real purpose of big sunglasses was to protect his face from being slapped by the offended bikinis at the beach.

Jorts

You dad wore jorts before you did and he's got the short frayed denim to prove it. Living the three Rs, he Reused his life-wrecked jeans by Reducing their leg length and Recycling them back into his wardrobe as stylish Danny Dukes. Now every pair of faded favorites could have a second life as his favorite pair of shorts.

SO HIPSTERS, next time you're riding a fixie in attire you claim is strictly functional because you can carry your keys and U-lock without having your leg movement constricted, remember this . . .

Your dad wore them because he was helping to save the environment before saving the environment was cool.

Mustaches

Your dad had a mustache before you did and he's got a warm upper lip to prove it. His homegrown facial bow tie was the envy-inducing expression of masculinity that confirmed his omega status within the manly community. Looking like two lost caterpillars on his face, that lower nose Picasso got him discounts at hardware stores, heavy machinery rental companies, and lumberyards.

SO HIPSTERS, when Movember rolls around and you're splashing Rogaine on your pathetic 'stache or dyeing it black with Just For Men to make it appear fuller, remember this . . .

Your dad has more testosterone then you will ever have and the proof is still sitting on his face.

Beards

Your dad had a beard before you did and his cheeks haven't seen the sun in years to prove it. Often mistaken for Sasquatch while in the woods, his face-fro was an unbridled expression of manhood. With it he could fell a tree without picking up an ax and stop bullets with its Kevlar-like strength. You know how your dad met your mom? His beard lured her in.

SO HIPSTERS, next time you're trying to grow your face in so that you look more masculine than you really are, remember this . . .

Your dad had the original beard to fear.

Unkempt Hair

Your dad had unkempt hair before you did and he has the snarled strands to prove it. Long before looking like you just rolled out of bed became fashionable, your dad's locks were just as out of control as he was. He didn't spend hours meticulously disheveling his hair with $40 product, he earned his look. His lengths were styled with motorcycle joyrides, fistfights, and a touch of "I don't give a fuck."

SO HIPSTERS, next time you're running your fingers through your nappy strands in front of a dirty mirror in your studio apartment, remember . . .

Your dad's hair made him look so gnar that people assumed he'd killed a man and gotten away with it.

Suspenders

Your dad wore suspenders before you did and his pants are secure to prove it. When your dad had a lady under each arm and two fistfuls of Bud at a dive bar, he needed a security system that ensured his slacks would stay where his hands couldn't keep them.

SO HIPSTERS, next time you're looking ironically Amish in the coffee shop while playing with your iPhone, remember this . . .

Your dad was so awesome that he had to strap clothes down to his body or they would explode off him.

Tank Tops

Your dad wore tank tops before you did and he's got the sunburnt shoulders to prove it. As the noncommittal middle ground of wearing or not wearing a chest covering, these shirts screamed summer harder than the bead of sweat dripping down the sunbathing backside of a Daisy Dukes–clad undergrad. He was a true follower of Bauhaus and lived a "less is more" lifestyle every time he slipped his slender frame into one of these lady magnets.

SO HIPSTERS, next time you're calling yourself Rave Heart while dancing the night away in your sweaty party tank, remember this . . .

Your dad was a tank in tops.

P.S. Your dad ironically ate luxury food when he was poor before you did too.

Ugly Sweaters

Your dad wore ugly sweaters before you did and he's got the embarrassing weavings to prove it. Since before Cosby was a prefix for it and parties were themed around it, your dad was rocking these glorious machine-knit pieces. His collection of knit Pollocks and wearable Warhols were the mullets of clothing, formal enough for work, yet wild enough to party in.

SO HIPSTERS, next time you're digging through the racks at the local thrift store looking for the perfect Cosby sweater for your annually unoriginal ugly Christmas sweater party, remember this . . .

Your dad's awesomeness poured into that sweater first and you're tainting the fibers that once touched greatness.

P.S. Sweaters + dance party = holy shit I can smell that hipster before I can see him.

Sideswept Hair

Your dad had sideswept hair before you did and he's got the bangs to prove it. Follicularly endowed, his tangles were the keystone of his killer style. Each strand was strategically placed to achieve optimum attraction. It was head art in motion and the legend of his locks was known in distant lands.

SO HIPSTERS, next time you're giving in-depth directions to a tattooed hair sculptor while sipping the free cheap beer included in your $40 cut, remember this . . .

Your dad is the reason why it's called a hair do instead of a hair don't.

Skinny Jeans

Your dad squeezed into skinny jeans before you did and he's lost the leg circulation to prove it. His physics-defying denim clung to his skin closer than ladies did to his side. Doctors could check his pulse by watching the rhythmic beat of cotton across his femoral artery and his pockets couldn't hold anything more than spare change.

SO HIPSTERS, next time you're struggling to get into a pair of 511s, remember this . . .

Your dad's jeans were so tight they make yours look baggy.

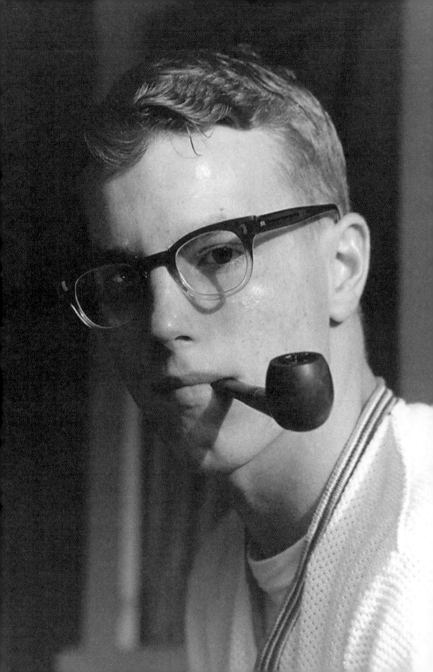

Thick-Framed Glasses

Your dad saw the world through thick-framed glasses before you did and he's got the bad eyesight to prove it. Functionally fashion-able, his prescribed sex appeal put his world in focus so he could shit-rip his way through life. They gave him an air of sophistication that even a PhD couldn't achieve.

SO HIPSTERS, when your box of Warby Parkers arrives and you're trying on the vintage-inspired eyewear that your perfect eyesight doesn't need, remember this . . .

Your dad earned those glasses by being authentically bad . . . at seeing.

Skinny Ties

Your dad kept his ties skinny before you did and he's got the pencil-thin collar accessory to prove it. His button coverer wasn't just a fashion statement, it was a functioning lover's leash that women used to lead him headlong back to their apartments.

SO HIPSTERS, when you're twisting your kite-rope-thin ties into minuscule knots to finish off your look for indie rock prom, remember this . . .

Your dad can still four-in-backhand your ass when you're being a douche.

Colored Knockoff Ray-Bans

Your dad wore neon sunglasses before you did and he's got the $10 knockoff Ray-Bans to prove it. Like a highlighter hugging his eye sockets, his shades were the awesome accent that made him stick out in a crowd. He was a life salmon that swam downstream when everyone else was trying to go up.

SO HIPSTERS, next time you're hating on the sun with lime green, purple, bright orange, or pink ray blockers that you bought at a gas station, remember this . . .

Your dad stood out, but you just stand in with the crowd.

Deep Vs

Your dad wore deep Vs before you did and he's got the plunging collars to prove it. He used his chest hair like a Venus flytrap for lady gazes and made them hotter than a Louisiana summer.

SO HIPSTERS, next time you're pulling on a neon American Apparel V-cut shirt, remember this . . .

Your dad was the only man who could ever tell a lady, "My eyes are up here."

Thrift Stores

Your dad thrifted before you did and he bought a $3 tweed over-coat with leather-patched elbows to prove it. Sifting through a basement of gently used, discarded fashion memories, he was a secondhand trendsetter and got dapper in the tax write-offs of the rich. He was less than wealthy back then, but his discerning bargain-hunting skills made it look like he lived on filet mignon.

SO HIPSTERS, when you're sniffing out garments at the local Goodwill in hunt of a perfectly ironic vintage T remember this . . .

Your dad was first at being second.

P.S. When people say you don't know a man until you've walked a mile in his shoes, they didn't mean you should go buy his shoes at Thrift Town. I'm sorry, that's gross.

Leather Jackets

Your dad wore leather jackets before you did and he's got the animal hide to prove it. He conditioned his trophy coat with whis-key spills, other men's blood, and 120-mph motorcycle wind-kisses. He was a kindred spirit with the sacrificed soul he bore on his back because, just like it, he was wild and untamed.

SO HIPSTERS, next time you're chest-deep in pleather, trying your hardest to look like you're not trying at all, remember this . . .

Your dad was the animal in the animal.

Sweatbands

Your dad wore a sweatband before you did and he's got the dry brow to prove it. Absorbing the awesomeness that poured from his being, his forehead ShamWow kept the saltwater sting from blurring his vision while he rocked it at basement shows.

SO HIPSTERS, when you're mashing your greasy locks under elasticized terry cloth because you secretly want to look like Richie Tenenbaum, remember this . . .

Your dad's sweatband served a purpose and made him look like he was ready to kick some ass, while yours only makes you look like you're ready to Jazzercise.

Fedoras

Your dad topped it with fedoras before you did and he knows where a killer haberdashery is to prove it. Unlike the 75 IQ baseball hat scarlet letters of the bro class, he insisted his headwear look as intelligent as he was. He could speak with his hat—a quick tip saluted fine honey dips and slight readjustments shunned half-wits.

SO HIPSTERS, next time you're trying to dress up your skull with something other than a beanie, remember this . . .

Your head's way too big to fit into your dad's kind of style.

Bow Ties

Your dad kept it crisp in bow ties before you did and he can still tie a knot so fresh that it would choke the pot smoke out of your throat to prove it. He was an office 007 with the fashion fortitude to pull off a neck dressing so bold that it would make most men look like pocket-protected lady repellers. But not your dad. Each elegant tangle of his collar-fixing further cemented his place in the dapper upper crust of the *GQ* elite.

SO HIPSTERS, next time you're watching a YouTube video on "how to tie a bow tie" while cursing furiously at how difficult this Rubik's Cube of fashion accessories is to solve, remember this . . .

Your dad killed it in the neck-knot game, but you'll always be only as genuine as a clip-on.

Jean Jackets

Your dad wore jean jackets before you did and he's got the Canadian tuxedo to prove it. His upper body quickly realized what his legs discovered first, that denim was the only fabric durable enough to withstand his Tasmanian devil lifestyle. So, with pants for a coat, he machine-gun–fisted his way through the years and never worried about tearing his style a new one.

SO HIPSTERS, when you're thrifting for the perfect preworn outerwear to sew your commercial rebellion patches onto, remember this . . .

Your dad styled his jean jacket with blood, grease, and bar fights, not needlepoint bullshit.

Women's Clothes

Your dad wore his girlfriend's clothes before you did and he's got the bare midriff to prove it. Looking like a flat-chested fourteen-year-old girl, he was the toughest chick most men got beat up by. Nearsighted construction workers gave him catcalls and he gave them fist-shadowed eye sockets in return. Once, while in West Hollywood, a blurry-eyed Steven Tyler sent him a drink from across a dark bar, the rest is "Dude looks like a lady" history.

SO HIPSTERS, next time you're shopping in your girlfriend's closet for the perfect pair of pants or buying Ex-Girlfriend Jeans from Levi's, remember this . . .

Your dad didn't have to get into women's pants to get into women's pants.

Mullets

Your dad rocked a mullet before you did and he had the beaver tail to prove it. When he was told that his long party locks weren't corporate enough, he trimmed nine to five into the front follicles and left the back as a joke. He never realized his actions would give birth to the first haircut with multiple personality disorder.

SO HIPSTERS, next time you're clipping the top of your hair short, shaving the sides, and ignoring the back like it's a Billboard top twenty track, then claiming it's "Euro," remember this . . .

Your dad was so influential that Europeans stole his hairstyle while vacationing in the States, made it popular abroad, and then had their version stolen back by Americans.

Flannel

Your dad flannelled it up before you did and he's got the Pendleton to prove it. Rivaled only by Paul Bunyan and the Brawny Man in masculinity, he was a man of the woods and his curated collection of finely woven wools was a lumberjack's dream. Each one of his shirts was pine-scented and broken in by ax-exploding logs into pieces.

SO HIPSTERS, when you're trying to look like the wilderness man you're not and you end up looking like a not-so-ironic version of Al Borland, remember this . . .

Flannel was created in your dad's image.

P.S. Smokey the Bear learned the hard way that you don't ask your dad to put out his cigar until he's finished.

Hoodies

Your dad hid in a hoodie before you did and he has evidence that the police once thought he was the Unabomber to prove it. Head buried deep in a drawstring hood, he looked like a 'stached societal menace that five-fingered store goods, spray-tagged buildings, and was just released on bail. But really, he was just cold.

SO HIPSTERS, when you're trying to conceal your beer belly and bedhead inside a hoodie while sipping fair-trade French press, remember this . . .

Your dad looked ominous in his hoodie, and you just look like a lost little boy who can't find his way home.

American Apparel

Your dad was into American Apparel before you and he's got the plain shirts to prove it. He was a monochromatic madman who didn't rep any brand other than his own. He knew all the Pantone numbers and looking into his dresser drawers was like looking into a kaleidoscope of fashion sense.

SO HIPSTERS, next time you're listening to Sleigh Bells in the dressing room while trying to look indifferent in the mirror, remember this . . .

Your dad inspired the store that millions of you find your basics at.

P.S. If millions of people shop at the same store, doesn't that make the store mainstream?

Peacoats

Your dad kept warm in a peacoat before you did and he has the anchor buttons to prove it. Long before you ever strolled into a surplus store to buy your own navy-issued bit of sex appeal, he was making blue wool look hot.

SO HIPSTERS, next time you're flipping up the collar on your stolen-style outerwear while smoking an American Spirit and looking indifferent to the climate, remember this . . .

Your dad is the reason cold looks hot.

P.S. Fat hipsters with beards who wear peacoats look like Paddington Bear.

Military Jackets

Your dad wore military-inspired jackets before you did and he's got the dog tags to prove it. He was a camo-clad deadeye that could bullet-kiss targets from more than a hundred yards away with his boomstick. With heightened senses and a tactically trained brain, he used his combat education to know when you were up to no good as a kid.

SO HIPSTERS, next time you're pulling on enlisted style with an ironic twist, remember this . . .

You'll always be a private compared to your dad, the General of Style.

Tube Socks

Your dad was foot-deep in tube socks before you were and he's got the stripes to prove it. He was the first one to show that even something deemed underwear could look cool. In his ankle-up version of skinny jeans, his legs were protected from the shin blows that life tried to throw at him while he kicked his way through it.

SO HIPSTERS, next time you're perfecting your Michael Cera in *Juno* look, remember this . . .

Your dad has been pulling up his socks since before you were pulling up your Huggies.

Members Only Jackets

My dad rocked Members Only jackets before I did and I found this exact jacket at his house a month ago to prove it (seriously, it's in the hall closet right next to his leather jacket). His secret society of swag was known for skinny jeans, ass-kicking, and thick lip-scarves. Contrary to conspiracy theorists' beliefs, the Freemasons, Illuminati, and Skull and Bones don't control the world; his jacket-clad man-lliance does. They've put presidents in office. They control the economy. And they taught me how to skate.

SO HIPSTERS, next time you're jacket-fronting like you're a real Member while walking around Williamsburg listening to indie playlists, remember this . . .

These coats actually stand for something other than irony when our dads wear them.

Hipster Offspring

Your dad made you a hipster before you could become one and he hand-selected the infant outfits to prove it. Fresh from the baby thrift store, he would dress you in the most dapper diaper coverings, hoping to nurture your pre–potty-trained fashion sense. A fun-sized Members Only jacket, baby's first Ray-Bans, skinny leggings, and of course, the knit hat—he always made sure you had the most ironic shrunk-down versions of hipster street couture.

SO HIPSTERS, next time you're curious about a fashion selection while eye-groping yourself in the mirror of a thrift store changing room, remember this . . .

You should call dad for advice because back in the day he made you the flyest baby in the sandbox.

Your dad did awesome shit . . .

Fact: Your dad did awesome shit back in the day.

He's done everything you've done but he did it better. His life resumé reads like a novel of dream-worthy proportions. Modern Renaissance men look untalented next to him while he made hard look easy and easy look effortless. He wasn't just a trendsetter, he was a global influencer who changed the world with the way he lived.

Filmmaking

Your dad was a filmmaker before you were and has a movie starring your mom to prove it. He was the Kubrick of domestic cinematography best known for the monumental documentaries *Baby's First Steps* and *Christmas 1985*, and the widely popular *Accidental Nut Shot: When Baseballs Strike Back*. While never reaching the drug-filled heights of Hollywood, his films can still be seen today on your local Betamax or VCR.

SO HIPSTERS, next time you're shooting HD video with your Flip cam or editing your shitty film noir with iMovie, remember this . . .

Your dad can still crossfade your ass with a flick of his wrist.

Riding a Motorcycle

Your dad rode a café racer before you did and he scarred the streets with rubber to prove it. His rebel yell was 120 decibels of gasoline-fueled mayhem. Armed with two wheels and clad in disobedience, he rode through the country leaving ringing eardrums as his calling card. He loved that bike and so did your mom. She would sing high notes of jubilee with every throttle pull that rumbled the seat beneath her.

SO HIPSTERS, next time you're saddled up to your motorized fixie, remember this . . .

You'll always ride bitch to your dad.

Sailing

Your dad was into sailing before you were and he's got the captain's hat to prove it. Riding his fixie of the sea, he sailed his boat like a fistfight and left black-eyed waves in his wake as a reminder to Poseidon that he was the true king of the depths. The Atlantic winds were his mistress, but your mom was the only woman who could raise his sail.

SO HIPSTERS, next time you're shopping for horizontal blue striped shirts, remember this . . .

You'll always just be a deckhand to the original master and commander.

Photography

Your dad was a photographer before you were and he's got the telephoto lens to prove it. He could set an f-stop with one hand while unhooking your mom's bra with the other. Like a 35mm ninja, he could slow his heart rate and steady his hands to the point where his body became the perfect tripod. And with surgical precision he opened the shutter to make moments last a lifetime.

SO HIPSTERS, next time you're snapping pics with your Diana or shooting shitty photos of your friends with a digital SLR in auto mode, remember this . . .

Your dad is the alpha dog of aperture.

P.S. Nobody gives a fuck what lens, flash, and film you used on an iPhone app to take that terrible photo of the vegan soy bullshit you're about to eat, so stop posting it on Facebook.

Big Headphones

Your dad had big headphones before you did and he still can't hear you because of it. His musical earmuffs were the world-silencing, pre-noise-canceling listening devices of choice. They let him enjoy Jimmy Page thrash a guitar solo without being interrupted by your guttural, ear-piercing screams that would have made Beethoven wish he was more deaf.

SO HIPSTERS, next time you're pulling on your headphones to listen to someone whine over bad chord progressions while you do poor typography on your shitty graphic designs, remember this . . .

Your dad's music was so seismic that earbuds couldn't contain it.

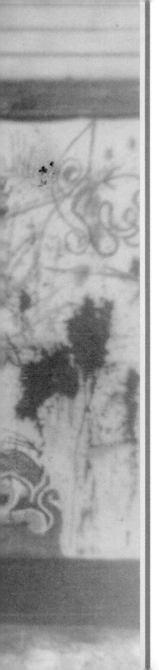

Art

Your dad was an artist before you were and he's got the brush skills to prove it. Drunk off creativity and high from huffing paint, he created inspired combinations of color and bristle strokes that would make Bob Ross give up his paints. He was the indie Van Gogh of the obscure art world and the Jimi Hendrix of the paint ax.

SO HIPSTERS, next time you're belly up to a canvas at liberal arts school, eye-gulping a naked dude and trying to re-create his form, remember this . . .

Your dad didn't need school to be a badass and he would have never painted man tackle.

Music Festivals

Your dad went to music festivals before you did and Woodstock had to go on a twenty-five–year hiatus as proof of it. He had the auditory honor of hearing Janis flex her choir muscles, experiencing Jimi shred, and witnessing the Grateful Dead come to life. It was a musical Mecca and he was one of the blessed few to make the pilgrimage.

SO HIPSTERS, next time you're bragging about how you saw Arcade Fire at Coachella or buying your choice substances for Burning Man, remember this . . .

Your dad's generation invented big summer blowouts and he can tell you how much beer to bring on your trip.

Riding a Fixie

Your dad rode a fixie before you did and he's got the blown-out knees to prove it. He was a velo Mad Max who lived in the in-between spaces of road, cars, and death. It took boulder balls to pedal recklessly when bike lanes were just unicorns and four-wheeled steel death dealers had no fear of letting him know who really owned the road. With every crank stroke, he poured bike freedom into pavement and reclaimed the streets from the tyranny of traffic.

SO HIPSTERS, when you're track standing at a stoplight or bustin' fixie tricks for bike gang groupies, remember this . . .

Your dad knew first not to brake what's already been fixed.

Guitar

Your dad played guitar before you did and he knows the progressions to prove it. He was a garage god that got shreddy on a Marshall half stack. Men envied his lightning-handed solos and women swooned at his acoustic sets. He was a six-string gunslinger and your mom was his first groupie.

SO HIPSTERS, next time you're trying to learn Elliott Smith's "Needle in the Hay" or some shitty Vampire Weekend song that your girlfriend heard on a TV commercial, remember this . . .

Your dad gave chords power.

Cats

Your dad was obsessed with cats before you were and he's been LOLing at them since pre-Internet times to prove it. He was a feline whisperer and one thing was for sure, wherever he went, pussy was sure to follow.

SO HIPSTERS, next time you're trolling cat memes at work or showing everyone photos of Boots your Persian something or other, remember this . . .

Your dad doesn't tolerate your bullshit, just like his cat.

Skateboard

Your dad rode a skateboard before you did and he has a picture in *Thrasher* to prove it. When your dad was younger, skateboarding was so underground that he had to build his own boards. The cops didn't know what to do with this new shit-kicking menace to the middle class, so they made skateboarding illegal.

SO HIPSTERS, next time you're obliviously rolling down the bike lane of some hipster neighborhood in SF, Portland, or New York, remember this . . .

Your dad was so awesome that the things he did for fun were made illegal in public places.

The Great Outdoors

Your dad was into Mother Nature before you were and he has the tent-popping skills to prove it. Scented with musk and adventure, your dad hiked cocksure into the wilderness with only his man-stincts and a few trusted supplies. He could fillet a fresh catch, intimidate a mountain lion, and start a fire with a glance.

SO HIPSTERS, next time you're packing up the 1990 Volvo wagon for a woodsy weekend escape from the bros who have overrun your parks remember this . . .

The great outdoors were just the outdoors until your dad got there.

Coffee

Your dad drank coffee before you did and he's got the stained teeth to prove it. He's been drinking since before Starbucks was a small Seattle coffee shop and long before you stopped drinking Starbucks because it was "too mainstream." His cups were a strong-handed, eye-jolting, bitch-slap to drowsiness. They kept the sleep-beast at bay so he could kill it in life each day.

SO HIPSTERS, next time you're stealing free Wi-Fi while sipping a fair-trade vanilla local roast splashed with soy bullshit and unrefined sugar, remember this . . .

Your dad only drank coffee that was like him, strong.

P.S. Your dad is so underground that he knows how to talk with the dead.

Vintage Bikes

Your dad was into old bikes before you were and he's got the lugs to prove it. He was a forefather of derailed speed and knew how to strip down more than just a bike frame. While everyone else was rocking Detroit muscle, he was repping chain-grease aftershave and bike-helmet cornrows.

SO HIPSTERS, next time you're dusting off his bike in the garage while home for Christmas from your liberal arts school and planning on stealing his vintage setup, remember this . . .

You'll always be training wheels to your dad's cycle swag.

Shooting Shit

Your dad was into shooting shit before you were and he has the gun-powder residue on his hands to prove it. Nothing says, "I'm going to tear shit up" like a pistol fully loaded with anarchy and aimed at the heart of fun. But that was when a man had to drink his twelve-ounce targets before he shot them. He was a deadeye with a BAC who only emptied clips from mountaintop firing ranges.

SO HIPSTERS, next time you're looking down the iron sights at the shooting range and acting like you're whiskey-steel-tough, remember this . . .

Your dad is why the seven-day waiting period was established.

Obscure Musical Instruments

Your dad played obscure musical instruments before you did and there's a sultry flute ballad about your mom to prove it. Everyone plays guitar; it's the English of musical languages and the instrument frat dogs pick up to woo women with unoriginality. Your dad was a true musician, a virtuoso of cylindrical steel and the pied piper of panty dropping.

SO HIPSTERS, next time you're red-eyed at an Edward Sharpe and the Magnetic Zeros concert and feeling mystically inspired to start playing the accordion or viola, remember this . . .

Your dad could give you obscure music lessons if he wasn't too busy working to pay for your liberal arts degree.

Photo Booths

Your dad knew about photo booths before you did and he has the consecutive stills to prove it. In the back of a smoke-filled dive bar, your dad first discovered these magic boxes of memories. Late one night after swilling down a whiskey, he asked for your mom's hand in photo infamy. He keeps their photo courtship in his wallet to this day.

SO HIPSTERS, next time you're filth-piling friends into a picture closet, trying to remember another night at the bar you always go to, remember this . . .

Your dad introduced you to the photo booth and you owe every one of your perfectly ironic drunken photo expressions to him.

Tall Bikes

Your dad rode tall bikes before you did and he's got the five-foot-high saddle to prove it. Like a mad scientist with a bachelor's degree in one-upsmanship and a minor in drunk cycling, he created the first two-wheeled Goliath whip. It defied logic, much like his life, and was the first Franken-ride the world had ever seen.

SO HIPSTERS, next time you're riding around atop two frames doggy-styling each other while acting like you don't care about the attention you're getting, remember this . . .

Your dad knew how to get high before you did, on bikes that is.

Typewriters

Your dad owned a typewriter before you did and he's got the white-out marks to prove it. His fingers punched keys and left black-eye alphabet marks on paper. However, it didn't leave squiggly red lines under his misspellings or grammatical slipups. It just did what he told it to, unlike you.

SO HIPSTERS, when you're getting back to the origins of being a writer and enjoying the rhythmic clack of mechanical type, remember this . . .

Those keys have seen words you can't even imagine, and your dad was the author.

P.S. The typewriter app for the iPad makes you look like a pretentious douche.

Non-American Sports

Your dad was into non-American sports before you were and he's got the juggling skills to prove it. While everyone else was chewing dip while playing first base, he was rainbow-kicking leather between goalposts. He lived for FIFA and got pissed during every game like all proper chaps do.

SO HIPSTERS, when you're watching the World Cup and cheering on the team from where you studied abroad, remember this . . .

Your dad could actually play the game, and can still nutmeg you to show he's the greatest.

Tattoos

Your dad had tattoos before you did and he still has the marks to prove it. Shoved deep beneath his skin were the rebel inkings of the anti-establishment. His arm art was the calling card of a bad boy who drew your innocent mom to his side. She was captivated by his adventures and smitten with the sense of danger that lingered around his body.

SO HIPSTERS, next time you're getting another part of your sleeve completed, remember this . . .

Your dad got all his tattoos in one sitting because he was man enough to endure five hours of being stabbed.

Ironically Played Sports

Your dad played sports ironically before you did and he's been banned from the country club to prove it. He couldn't afford the greens fees, so, with his hitting sticks tossed over his shoulder, he was the B&E master of back-nine robberies. His ten handicap was earned while outrunning golf-cart security forces and pond diving for "new" golf balls. While his attire wasn't traditionally acceptable, he showed the polos that cutoffs had their place at the links.

SO HIPSTERS, next time you're thinking about hitting up eighteen holes with a 24-pack of High Life because alt-golf is the new bike polo, remember this . . .

Your dad was a lady killer on the links long before Tiger picked up his woods.

Barbecue

Your dad knew how to BBQ before you did and he's got the lighter-fluid skills to prove it. He vigilantly manned his beast cooker and never burnt a meal. Taste buds sang his praises and his culinary wizardry single-handedly inspired the Food Network to become a TV station.

SO HIPSTERS, when you're patio-cooking smug vegan burgers and local veggies while downing tallboys and getting terrible tan lines, remember this . . .

Your dad will slow-cook your ass if you ever touch his grill.

Portable Music Players

Your dad had a portable music player before you did and he's got the sore arms to prove it. With two five-inch speakers and four D batteries, he was a street DJ that shoulder-rocked blocks with his tape-deck picks.

SO HIPSTERS, when you're filling your iPod with indie tunes and making playlists for your morning subterranean commutes, remember this . . .

Your dad literally had to carry his music everywhere he went.

Read Everything

Your dad read everything before you did and he has the collection of first editions to prove it. This flannel-clad Kerouac consumed language with a ferocity only rivaled by Merriam-Webster. The written word was an obsession and his free hours were spent getting copiously intoxicated off the eloquent arrangements of literary demigods.

SO HIPSTERS, next time you're quoting a Faulkner passage from your perfectly curated library, remember this . . .

Your dad read it first and he summoned that poetically penned prose to wobble women's knees.

P.S. How can you hipsters call yourself intellectuals when your actions help breed the biggest bastard children known to the English language, textspeak and emoticons? You pricks.

Eating Local

Your dad ate locally before you did and he's got the dirt under his fingernails to prove it. He gardened because he wanted to, not because it was trendy. His plate was always filled with the kind of goodness that only comes from being homegrown.

SO HIPSTERS, when you're asking the waitress if the tomatoes in your salad are ethically grown, locally produced, fair trade, and sustainable, and if the workers were given a livable wage, remember this . . .

Your dad didn't eat local so that he could have another thing to be pretentious about, he ate it because he knew it tasted better.

Esoteric Interests

Your dad had esoteric interests before you did and he's thrown the clay to prove it. When he wasn't stealing other men's girls, he was the Don Juan of intellectual pursuits. He was a Renaissance man who was a natural at being a natural.

SO HIPSTERS, when you're learning needlepoint or getting into early French noir cinema, remember this . . .

Your dad had a lot of obscure hobbies, but you've probably never heard of them.

Video Games

Your dad played video games before you did and he has the three-letter trophies to prove it. Back then, the arcade was where boys were chiseled into legendary men. Your mom was there too, along with the rest of the local talent pool, and they would peer over his shoulder and swoon in awe at the precision with which he commanded the sticks.

SO HIPSTERS, next time you're sitting in the back of a dive bar feeding your laundry funds into a game with dreams of being the next King of Kong, remember this . . .

That's your dad's high score on every arcade game you've ever played and no one has been able to dethrone him in more than twenty years.

Mopeds

Your dad rode a moped before you did and then he stopped. He realized that these two-wheeled lady-repellers were the training wheel equivalent of the motorcycle world. Training wheels won't get you laid. But he knew he had to learn how to ride somehow and this motorized starter bike was how he did it.

SO HIPSTERS, next time you're riding a Puch with your "gang" and wearing cutoff jean jackets hoping to pick up little hipster diddies, remember this . . .

Unlike you, your dad looked badass even on a scooter.

Synth

Your dad was into synth before you were and he's made the electric beats to prove it. He was a sorcerer of electric dance magic and cast beat spells over the masses, making party sirens gyrate till the wee hours of the morning.

SO HIPSTERS, when you're rolling to dubstep in a dirty warehouse club at 3 A.M., remember this . . .

Your dad's beats shook the room before anyone had even heard of electronica.

Apple Computers

Your dad owned an Apple before you did and he's got the Macintosh Classic to prove it. Back when Steve Jobs was a mere mortal, your dad was a keystroke king of Cupertino. He could command-option and control-shift shortcuts while flipping floppies. Flying the rebel rainbow was in his blood and he's been part of the Mac army since before PCs knew there was a fight.

SO HIPSTERS, when you're anxiously awaiting the next Macworld keynote while showing off your bitten apple brand-marked skin and looking down on PC owners for defiling the free Wi-Fi with their laptops, remember this . . .

Your dad can still command Z your ass if you step out of line.

Your dad knew how to live . . .

Contrary to the aged image that is your current perspective of your dad, he was an animal back in the day. He rose each morning with greater force than the sun and filled his days with enough living for two men.

He knew the best places to hang out.

He worked shitty jobs to support his weekend partying.

He drank cheap beer till last call and got kicked out of bars.

He told people exactly how he felt and didn't give a fuck.

He traveled the world and experienced everything in it.

So, next time you're looking at your dad, know that there is still a hell beast inside his now time-tamed body that lived every moment of life to the fullest.

Being Apathetic

Your dad was apathetic before you were and he doesn't even care that I'm writing about him to prove it. He didn't care that it was balls-soup–hot outside because he was still going to wear flannel at the lake. He didn't care that your mom was wearing a boat-capsizing bikini or that there was a giant waterslide filled with fun sitting to his right. Hell, if Loch Ness herself rose from the murky depths and tried to bum a Parliament out of his pack, he still wouldn't leave his lawn chair of lakeside luxury.

SO HIPSTERS, next time you're talking in monotone about the show you might or might not go see tonight while avoiding eye contact, remember this . . .

Your dad could have been king shit of apathy had he cared enough to become it.

Dating Women Out of His League

Your dad dated women out of his league before you did and his friends are still confused about how he pulled it off. Sexy like a plumber and described as "unique" at best by his buddies, women still couldn't resist him. He was a Navy SEAL of seduction who tactically disarmed biddies with quiet confidence and a comedic wit.

SO HIPSTERS, when you're drinking liquid courage to approach a local ten-point while trying to convince your skinny-jean–clad friend to help you out, remember this . . .

Your dad was his own wingman.

Hanging Out on Rooftops

Your dad hung out on rooftops before you did and he can still climb a fire escape to prove it. Screw parks, he knew those places were the bro football fields/family picnic hot spots/dog toilets of the city. That's why he set his sights higher to the untouched peaks of the city skyline. Each night it transformed into his urban observatory for starry sky gazing and it was the first place he showed your mom the Big Dipper.

SO HIPSTERS, next time you're looking over the edge of a building, holding back the urge to spit off it while drinking tallboys of Tecate, remember this . . .

Your dad knew rooftops were the best place to look down on people first.

Nonconformist

Your dad wasn't mainstream before you weren't and he's been hated on to prove it. Instead of stealing from the past and remixing the already used up, he time-traveled his style from the future and was so fresh that it took twenty years for the rest of the world to catch up.

SO HIPSTERS, next time you're rejecting society's norms and basing your life around everything everyone else isn't doing, remember this . . .

Your dad is so ahead of the game that your kids will be wearing what he's rocking right now.

Not Smiling

Your dad didn't smile before you didn't and he's got an aggro-looking photo to prove it. He knew expressing feelings of joy with facial muscles took away from the air of hardness he had so painstakingly created. Muggers avoided him because he looked like a man who could bury an assailant without scuffing his business casual fresh kicks.

SO HIPSTERS, next time you're not expressing joy because everything is terrible in your middle-class–funded, want-for-nothing lifestyle, remember this . . .

Your dad was the master of fierce-face and it kept you safe as a baby.

Being a Grown-Ass Child

Your dad was a man-child before you were and he's still got the playground skills to prove it. He knew that growing up was for suckers. While time tried to thwart his fun, this human T. Rex refused to let it. He blew shit up with fireworks, played video games, and got wrecked off whiskey.

SO HIPSTERS, next time you're calling for more money because you blew all your cash on kombucha and cappucinos, remember this . . .

Your dad might have been young at heart but he was still a responsible, contributing member of society when he had to be.

I wish I could say the same for you.

San Francisco

Your dad repped Frisco before you did and he's got the leg muscles to prove it. In a land of misfit toys and hippie burnouts, your dad was a local. Like every good SF hipster, he lived in the Mission. He rode the 49, was sketched out by the 16th Street BART stop, and knew the fog rolling over Twin Peaks marked the beginning of night. He day-drank in Dolores Park, hated on the Marina, and was smugger than the exhaust note of a Prius.

SO HIPSTERS, when you're arguing who has the best burrito, sipping Four Barrel, or sweating the night away at Public Works, remember this . . .

Your dad probably partied and defiled every Mission house you've ever set foot in.

P.S. Hipster street cred points if you know where this photo was taken.

P.P.S. Taqueria Cancun is the jam and I'll argue anyone who doesn't think it's the best.

Being Skinny

Your dad was skinny before you were and he's got the scale readings to prove it.

But unlike you, he didn't have to go on the daily hipster diet of fixie rides, half packs of cigarettes, and piss-warm PBR. He just lived. Instead of sitting in front of a Mac trying to discover new bands, he was out body-rocking to alt bands in basement bars. Slenderness was the result of his ass-kicking, calorie-punching lifestyle.

SO HIPSTERS, next time you're struggling to get into your skinny jeans, remember this . . .

You're dad made lean mean.

Working Shitty Jobs

Your dad worked shitty jobs before you and he has the Kmart name tag to prove it. His hourly wage was less than a can of beer a hour and society used him as a bitching post for its corporate complaints. But even though his job was shit, he still managed to be the shit. Every Friday night he shed his 2-x-4 name badge of shame and was king of the weekend.

SO HIPSTERS, next time you're complaining to your parents about how you can't make rent because those damn mainstream yuppies don't tip you at the coffee shop, remember this . . .

Your dad knows about living hand-to-mouth and he drank PBR because it was all he could afford, not because it was ironic.

Judging People

Your dad judged people before you did and he can point out everything wrong with you to prove it. Casting more judgment than Judy and picking out character flaws like a social plastic surgeon, your dad made the callouts that destroyed top-forty trend followers.

SO HIPSTERS, when you're throwing looks of "I can't believe that fashion hack is wearing relaxed-fit Levi's" while smoking an American Spirit and commenting on how inhaling anything other than natural tobacco is bad for you, remember this . . .

Your dad is judging you right now because in your attempt to be the most original creation in the universe you've become the one thing you've been rebelling against for years: him.

Not Giving a Fuck

Your dad didn't give a fuck before you didn't and he's saddled up a porcelain throne in the woods to prove it. His soul was ungoverned by the oppressive chains of appropriateness and he did whatever the hell he wanted. He pissed in the wind of life and was a Renaissance man of living the High Life.

SO HIPSTERS, when you're getting drunk on a school night or trying to ignore how many people hate you on the Internet, remember this . . .

You're the offspring of a man for whom modern laws were put in place to stop.

Bro Bashing

Your dad bro-bashed before you did and he's thrown his back out mockingly lifting weights to prove it. He was a lion tamer of douche who could un-pop a collar with a comment and bitch-slap graphic Ts off backs with his banter. Each night he prowled the streets performing a magnum opus of boot-cut, gelled-hair hate.

SO HIPSTERS, next time you're mocking the athletic asshole in an Easter-pink collared shirt and flip-flops, remember this . . .

Your dad invented the label bro as a derogatory term first and those modern pea-brained cavemen adopted it because they were too stupid to realize it wasn't a good thing to be.

Shitty Apartments

Your dad had a shitty apartment before you did and had a rat friend named Jerry to prove it. Smelling like bar-floor runoff, he filled his casa with the abandoned street children of the furniture world and freebies deemed not fit to sit on by family members. It was a beer bottle maze with a laundry hamper floor and mystery-stained carpet. When he moved, the landlord condemned the whole damned complex.

SO HIPSTERS, next time you're scratching your bedbug war wounds or party-rocking stains into the floor, remember this . . .

Your dad is the reason security deposits exist.

Self-Portraits

Your dad took self-portraits before you did and he was the man in the mirror to prove it. With his lens gazing deep into the looking glass, he immortalized his image on every roll of his 35mm film. These were single-shot warnings to film techs that said, "This is the man you have to face if you mess up the film."

SO HIPSTERS, next time you're having an iPhone bathroom-mirror photo shoot for your Facebook profile pic, remember this . . .

Your dad could intimidate from an image.

Was Chuck Norris

Your dad was Chuck Norris before Chuck Norris was and he has the gun-shot wound to the face to prove it. Before *Walker, Texas Ranger* graced our idiot boxes with his kung fu moves, tight jeans, and justice, your dad was out there taking care of the streets. Law? He was the law. He worked for the LAPD back when just thinking about Los Angeles could get you killed. But every day this real-life badass put on his badge and kicked the shit out of those streets.

SO HIPSTERS, next time you're coming up with a Chuck Norris fact, remember this . . .

Your dad makes Chuck Norris flinch.

Protesting

Your dad protested before you did and he's got the police record to prove it. Fighting for better pay, equal rights, and to end a war, his megaphone blasted his voice box so the world knew what he thought was wrong with it. Nothing could stop him from flexing his freedom of speech. Your mom joined him too—she burned her bra after he helped her take it off.

SO HIPSTERS, next time you're protesting for more bike lanes in Williamsburg or showing support for some obscure human rights group, remember this . . .

Your dad had something real to fight for.

Looking Homeless

Your dad looked homeless before you did and he's got the spare change to prove it. After twelve fingers of whiskey and four hands of Hamm's, he often found temporary street beds when his legs couldn't carry him home. His disheveled appearance single-handedly spawned the term "homeless chic." He always woke up to generous donations with a rested smile on his face. The local hobos never knew he wasn't one of them.

SO HIPSTERS, next time you drunkenly pass out on public transit and find your likeness plastered on hipsterorhomeless.com the next day, remember this . . .

If it weren't for your dad's weekly deposits into your bank account, you'd actually be out on the streets and the only sign you'd be worthy of holding is: "Will look apathetic for food."

Photobombing

Your dad photobombed before you did and his friends have the pictures to prove it. He was a 4-x-6 asshole who, with facial contortions and well-timed leaps, ruined 35mm memories. It wasn't until days after the shot, when the photos had been developed, that innocent bystanders realized their portraits had been vandalized by a deranged-looking stranger.

SO HIPSTERS, next time you spot a group of girls ready to commemorate the night out and you're thinking about crashing their fun by face-diving into their photo, remember this . . .

Your dad exploded into pictures with his entire being and that is why it's called a photoBOMB.

Being More Intelligent Than Other People

Your dad knew he was smarter than other people before you did and he's got the awards to prove it. His thought-box fired at bullet speed and ran mental marathons around the ill-equipped minds that surrounded him. With his dictionary-sized vocabulary, he word-beat smart people into feeling stupid without even trying.

SO HIPSTERS, when you're treating someone like a second-class citizen and spewing off facts you just looked up on your phone, remember this . . .

Your dad was a human Wikipedia of knowledge before the Internet was even a thing.

Hating on Everything

Your dad hated on everything before you did and he knows the sign language to prove it. Wrapped in the First Amendment, he let his middle finger catch breezes like a Cadillac's hood ornament. His tongue was sharpened from verbal battles against everything that chapped his ass, which was a lot of things considering his shorts could barely cover a back cheek. But even though he was filled with venomous spit and fiery blood, there was one thing he couldn't hate: your mom.

SO HIPSTERS, next time you're sitting in a coffee shop with your cohort of cronies and discussing why everyone else in the room sucks, remember this . . .

Your dad had the balls to hate in public, not behind people's backs.

Shitty Cars

Your dad had a shitty car before you did and he's got the mechanic skills to prove it. With a Bondo body and duct-tape window seals, his chariot was less than glorious. It did 0-to-60 mph in 3.5 . . . minutes that is. It was more of a rolling backseat than a mode of transportation, which is exactly why he bought it.

SO HIPSTERS, when your 1989 Volvo wagon with 160,000 miles is in the shop yet again, remember this . . .

Your dad broke in your car long before you had a license.

Traveling the Globe

Your dad traveled the globe before you did and his band has the world tour T-shirts to prove it. He didn't need to know the local dialect because he spoke cross-cultural body sign language. As an ambassador of badassery, he jet-setted the world and left a wake trail of debauchery at every stop.

SO HIPSTERS, next time you're planning a summer abroad on dad's dime and claiming that it's necessary for you in order "to find yourself," remember this . . .

Your dad would come visit you in Europe, but he partied so hard that he's not legally allowed back into certain countries.

Looking Like Jesus

Your dad looked like Jesus before you did and he's got the "I just spent forty days and forty nights fasting in the desert" look to prove it. Unlike his biblical doppelgänger, he couldn't turn water into a good time or create vegan, fair-trade, organic loaves of bread from rocks. Instead, like a drunk savior of the party masses, he gave cheap beer to the thirsty and opened fully shaken PBR blessings on the dance floor. While he never cured the sick, he did cure the sober.

SO HIPSTERS, next time you're walking past a church and someone does a double take, remember this . . .

Your dad was mistaken for the second coming first.

P.S. You're not an immaculate conception.

Not Looking at the Camera

Your dad didn't look at the camera for photos before you didn't and he's got the "deep" shots to prove it. Women were like moths to his flame when they saw his 4-x-6s and never realized his inattentive stares were intentional.

SO HIPSTERS, next time you're striking a side pose and trying to plan a shot that looks unplanned, remember this . . .

Your dad learned how to ignore the camera from years of ignoring you.

Refusing to Participate

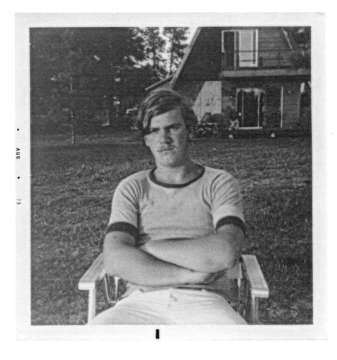

Your dad didn't participate in things before you didn't and he's never been on a team to prove it. He was a one-man wolf pack who hated on everything organized. He walked his own path in life and it was always where no one else was headed.

SO HIPSTERS, when you're intentionally avoiding fun situations where you might be asked to join in, remember this . . .

You dad was down to participate in one thing and you wouldn't be here if he didn't.

Chicago

Your dad lived in Chicago before you did and he had the Logan Square address to prove it. He stood on the Blue Line, party-rocked the Smart Bar at the Metro, and ate the tacos that inspired Flash Taco. His nights didn't end until the after-hours bars kicked him out, and he tolerated Chi-Town winters because he knew the summers were that gold.

SO HIPSTERS, when you're sitting in your Bucktown or Wicker Park apartment and hating on the Lincoln Park bro crowd while sipping Intelligentsia coffee, remember this . . .

Your dad has been getting slammed on Old Style since before you were slamming baby bottles.

Swearing

Your dad swore a lot before you did and he tagged the F-bomb to prove it. He was a connoisseur of cuss who could use bold words in ways you've never imagined. Not limiting himself to just the present, past, and future tenses, he could slam down an exclamation point swear in adverb, noun, adjective, and even past participle forms.

SO HIPSTERS, when you're verbally taking a small child's innocence with your careless use of hard language, remember this . . .

Your dad wrote the AP Stylebook on "fuck."

Drinking Cheap Beer

Your dad drank cheap beer before you did and he's had the spins to prove it. With a PBR-soaked liver, Hamm's-filled blood, and Keystoned eyes, he lived the High Life while kicking it Old Style. These party pints were his go-to drink of drunk that kept him swimming in a sea of buzz until last call.

SO HIPSTERS, next time you're chugging a tallboy of Tecate while sweatin' it at '90s night, remember this . . .

Your dad is the reason Milwaukee's Best is called The Beast.

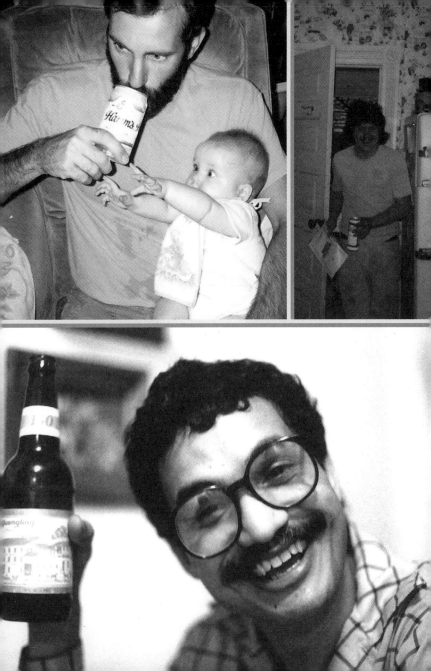

Day Drinking

Your dad got day-drunk before you did and he took the post-afternoon recovery naps to prove it. Like an inebriated Einstein, he solved the theory of relative intoxication, thus shifting the socially acceptable hours of "smashed" into the previously responsible hours of daytime. Now the party started when he said it did, which happened to be at 1 P.M. on a Tuesday some days.

SO HIPSTERS, when you're sitting in a city park on a sunny Saturday and drinking a High Life, remember this . . .

Your dad was a wasted genius and we all owe him a debt of gratitude for teaching us that sunlight makes beer taste better.

Having a Crusty Group of Friends

Your dad had a group of crusty friends before you did and your grandparents were afraid to leave him alone because of it. Just shy of being considered a gang by the local law, this friendship hurricane was notorious for its debaucherous acts. They crashed parties, killed kegs, and gave back-alley beat-downs to anyone who looked at them wrong. They were more than just a man clan, they were your dad's family.

SO HIPSTERS, next time you're rolling six-deep to a party you weren't invited to and then getting kicked out for being assholes, remember this . . .

Your dad and his friends didn't go to parties, they were parties.

Theme Parties

Your dad went to theme parties before you did and he's got the dress-up skills to prove it. Bored with mundane house ragers, he channeled the Halloween spirit in July and threw the first non-October costume bash in the history books. He had unintentionally unearthed party gold and was labeled a creative visionary of crunk.

SO HIPSTERS, next time you're 8-bit rocking a Mario Brothers theme party or slow dancing at your ironic prom, remember this . . .

Your dad didn't Google steal-search themes because his brain was warped enough to come up with his own.

DJing

Your dad was a DJ before you were and he can still beat match better than you to prove it. He pumped furious alt beats across pirate airwaves and blasted indie LPs at 11. While he might have had a face for radio, his voice was a celebrity on the streets.

SO HIPSTERS, next time you're spinning on the 1s and 2s under the name Party Wizard while trying to get it hyphy, remember this . . .

Your dad was a real DJ, a disc jockey, and your MacBook couldn't touch his turntables.

Smoking

Your dad smoked before you did and he knows how to hold a butt to prove it. Back when it was healthy and laws didn't prohibit it, your dad made addiction look cool with every exhale. He French-inhaled, blew smoke-ring love to your mom, and lit up anywhere he damn well pleased.

SO HIPSTERS, next time you're puffing a P-Funk while taking a break from the job you don't really do, remember this . . .

Your dad gave up lung darts once he discovered ladies don't like ashtray kisses.

Craft Beers

Your dad was into craft beer before you were and he has one of the best breweries around to prove it. He was the MacGyver of making drunk, the Mozart of all things malt. He could bottle a beer with one hand, seduce your mother with the other, and still never spill a drop.

SO HIPSTERS, next time you belly up to the bar, scratching your beard and staring at the tap selection like it was a vintage vinyl collection, remember this . . .

Your dad knew beer before you did and you can taste his knowledge on your local tap by ordering a Bell's.

P.S. Thank you Larry Bell for brewing one of my favorite beers. I tip my cycling cap to you and raise my pint of Oberon.

Pre-gaming

Your dad pre-gamed before you did and he's never showed up at a bar sober to prove it. Unlike his three-beer friends who got buzzed from looking at bottles, he had a man-sized tolerance. His liver deserves a Purple Heart for the tours of duty it served under his command.

SO HIPSTERS, when you're slamming drinks before you head out because you're too poor to pay for them at the bar, remember this . . .

Your dad always started the party before the party even started.

Raging

Your dad knew how to rage before you did and his friends are still afraid to give him whiskey because of it. At about half past tipsy, the quiet giant bear-child awoke from his sober slumber and became a shit-ripping, F5 party tornado.

SO HIPSTERS, next time you're recounting a tale of intoxicated past and bragging about how awesome you were last night, remember this . . .

Your dad is the patron saint of partying and the reason the term "that guy" exists.

Special Thanks

I owe a lot of people a thank-you for everything they have done for me over the years that helped make this book possible. Thank you to both my parents; you've done more for me than I could have ever asked for. Thank you to all my friends who've shown their support. Thank you to The Brandcenter and the professors. Thank you to Coz and Charles; I wouldn't be the writer I am today if it weren't for you two. And finally, thank you to Evan, Neil, and Alec for supporting me and for keeping me grounded.

Thank You, Dad

I owe my dad the biggest thank-you of all. He was my inspiration for this book and he truly is an amazing man. He gave up a lot so that I could have a great life. I've never wanted for anything and he gave me more than I ever could have asked for. He didn't just raise me, he taught me how to be a real man. I can honestly say that I wouldn't be where I am today if it wasn't for him. He believed in me when I didn't believe in myself. He picked me up when life knocked me down and was there for me each time I screwed up. He's more than just a dad, he's my mentor and one of my best friends. I hope one day that I will be half the dad he is because even if I was only half, I know I would still be an awesome dad.

I know I don't say this enough, Dad, but I love you and thank you for everything that you've ever done for me. I am truly grateful and blessed to have you as my dad.

Photo Credits

Front cover photo by Ron Thorne-Finch.

Page 6: Sophie Merry (Dad: Brian Merry); Page 7: Justine Benanty (Dad: Charles B.); Page 8: Kelly Ryan (Dad: Kevin Ryan); Page 9: Julia Good (Dad: Dale Good); Page 10: Eric Sams (Dad: Jerry Sams); Page 11: Susanne Taylor (Dad: Robin Taylor); Page 12: Allison Lucy (Dad: Scott Lucy); Page 13: Kate Hodges (Dad: Billy Letcher); Page 14 (top): Brooke Hawkins (Dad: Bob Hawkins); Page 14 (bottom): Secia Mischke (Dad: Perry Stephens); Page 15 (top): Lauren Gwaley (Dad: David Ashley Gwaley); Page 15 (bottom left): Stacie and Brad Goodman (Dad: Steve Goodman); Page 15 (bottom right): John Woods (Dad: Jack Woods); Page 16: Isreal Lawrence (Dad: Steven Lawrence); Page 17: Jay Milisavljevic (Dad: Milan Milisavljevic); Page 18: Sara Curtin (Dad: Jim Curtin); Page 19: Erin May Thompson Deprez (Dad: Lee Michael Thompson); Page 20: Mollie Davis (Dad: Rick Davis); Page 21: Jess Horwitz (Dad: Bob Horwitz); Page 22: Devin Rice (Dad: Dixon Bennett Rice, Jr.); Page 24: Matt, Brad, and Jason Getty (Dad: Larry Getty); Page 25: Lynae Zebest (Dad: Frank Straw); Page 26: Elizabeth Buckler (Dad: James R Buckler); Page 29: Rochelle Ask (Dad: Mickey Ask); Page 30: Dario Luca Utichi (Dad: Claudio Utichi); Page 31: Mary Zezza (Dad: David C. Zezza Jr.); Page 32: Emily Johnson (Dad: Buzz); Page 33: David Rosen; Page 35: Brie Martin (Dad: Dale Martin); Page 36: Anonymous; Page 37: Emma Roy (Dad: Jimmy Roy); Page 39: Emily Buckler (Dad: Bill Buckler); Page 40: Rachel Hermann (Dad: Patrick Hermann); Page 41 (top): Jenn Fenn (Dad: Dale Edward Fenn); Page 41 (bottom left): Karina Cochran (Dad: Steve Cochran); Page 41 (bottom right): Lauren Downing (Dad: Hugh Downing); Page 42: Lisa MacLarty (Jay MacLarty); Page 43: Hattie Stewart (Dad: Chris Stewart); Page 44: Rima; Page 46: Shannon Sallee (Dad: Mark Sallee); Page 47: Allison Harvey (Dad: Tom Harvey); Page 48: Matt, Brad, and Jason Getty (Dad: Larry Getty); Page 49: Ashlee Petty (Dad: Mike Petty); Page 52: Katherine Rainone (Dad: Ronald Rainone); Page 53: Dean Steven Waldron (Dad: Mark Alan Waldron); Page 54: (top): Cast of Vices; Page 54 (bottom): Jake Hawkes; Page 55: (top): Jaimie Wallace (Dad: William Wallace); Page 55 (bottom): Abby Dreier (Dad: Roy Dreier); Page 56: Lauren Cawdrey (Dad: Pat Abbe); Page 58: Katie Marchant (Dad: Richard Anthony Smith); Page 59: Erin Landry (Dad: Robert Landry); Page 60: Matthew Davis (Dad: Mark Davis); Page 62: Lydia Braam (Dad: Dennis Braam); Page 63: Katherine Clancy Leitner (Dad: Boyd Fink); Page 64: Anonymous; Page 65: Matt, Brad, and Jason Getty (Dad: Larry Getty); Page 67: Jennifer Helwich-Watanabe (Dad: Rudy Helwich); Page 68: Lucas Eaton; Page 69: Jeff White (Dad: Rick Vaningan); Page 70: Sam Rosen (Dad: Jay Rosen); Page 71: Rachel Harkai; Page 72: Erin Friedmann (Dad: Daniel Friedmann); Page 74: Ithyle Griffiths; Page 75: Bryan Zera (Dad: Steve Zera); Page 76: Rachel Reiff Ellis (Dad: Joe Reiff); Page 78: Natalie O' Sullivan (Dad: John O'Sullivan); Page 79: Courtney Cox (Dad: Matt Cox); Page 80: Marcus Siegel (Dad: Larry Siegel); Page 81: Lisa Pritchard; Page 82: Sarah Schwartz (Dad: Ron Schwartz); Page 84: Anonymous; Page 85: Chris Freeman (Dad: Robert Freeman); Page 86: Nathanael Cameron (Dad: Gary Cameron); Page 87: Kathleen Canavan (Dad: Bob Canavan); Page 88: Erin Thompson (Dad: Robert Thompson); Page 90: Deidra Castillo (Dad: Jim Castillo); Page 91: Nathan Puckett (Dad: Gary Puckett); Page 94: Dayena Campbell (Dad: Ken Campbell); Page 95: Kirsten Donk; Page 96: Sean Jones; Page 97: Gwyneth Perry (Dad: William Perry); Page 98: Kristina Moore (Dad: Tom Moore); Page 99: Jessie Atkinson (Dad: Tom Heffernan); Page 100: Ben Lempert (Dad: Chuck Lempert); Page 101: Jessica Voight (Dad: Danny Voight); Page 102: Amy Miller (Dad: Doug Miller); Page 103: Briana Milman; Page 104: Bridget Buckley (Dad: John E Buckley); Page 105: Michael Pambos; Page 106: Andrea Marie Lipp (Dad: Jonathan Marshall Lipp); Page 107: Caitlin S. Weigel (Dad: Kevin L. Weigel); Page 108: Emily Birkeland (Dad: Eric Birkeland); Page 109: Jade Neville (Dad: Gary Neville); Page 110: Daniel Medina Cleghorn (Dad: Enrique Medina); Page 112: Helen Hoepfner (Dad: Gregory Hoepfner); Page 113: Alison Calais (Dad: Steven Calais); Page 114: Kellie Gibson (Dad: Jim Gibson); Page 115: Ginny Braud (Dad: Kenny Braud); Page 116: Ryan Gratzer (Dad: Alan Gratzer); Page 117: Nicholas Mathis (Uncle: Jerry Howerton); Page 119: Neil Slotterback (Dad: Tom Slotterback); Page 120: Jenny Hasenfuss (Dad: Richard Hasenfuss); Page 121: Anna Konya (Dad: John Konya); Page 122: Edie Joseph; Page 123: Matt Wallace (Dad: Jeffrey V. Wallace); Page 124 (top): Nick Giberti (Dad: Steve Giberti); Page 124 (bottom left): Brianna Prahl; Page 125 (top left): Ashley Jean Hight; Page 125 (top right): Lindsay Chamberlain (Dad: Brad Chamberlain); Page 125 (bottom): Peter Roldan (Dad: Julian Roldan); Page 126: Tyler White; Page 127: Eddie Austin; Page 128: Emily Piper-Phillips (Dad: Steve Piper); Page 129: Lindsay Riley (Dad: Bill Riley); Page 130: Charlotte Green (Dad: Tom Green); Page 131: Laura Bell (Dad: Larry Bell); Page 132: Nicky Devine (Dad: David "Harry" Devine); Page 133: Kevin Fergus; Page 134: Matt, Brad, and Jason Getty (Dad: Larry Getty).

Library of Congress Cataloging-in-Publication
Data:
Getty, Brad.
  Dads are the original hipsters / Brad Getty.
    p. cm.
  ISBN 978-1-4521-0885-8
  1. Fathers—Humor. 2. Fathers—Pictorial
works. I. Title.

PN6231.F37G48 2012
818'.602—dc23

                        2011037156

Manufactured in China
Designed by Allison Weiner

10 9 8 7 6

Chronicle Books LLC
680 Second Street
San Francisco, California 94107
www.chroniclebooks.com